PUNK S

THE *Intergalactic,* **SUPERMASSIVE**

SPACE BOOK

The Punk Science team lives and works in the Science Museum. They spend their days performing experiments of all shapes and sizes and on the odd occasion performing science shows.

Jon Milton is the fearless and clueless leader of the team. He's always ready with a plan — it's not always a good one, but it is a plan nonetheless. He likes experiments that help him with his hobbies of flying and scuba-diving. By hobbies we actually mean things he'd like to do if he wasn't so lazy.

Dan Hope is the ultimate guitar-playing action hero (he thinks!). Unfortunately for him his action-hero status doesn't go any further than his head — not even a little bit into his neck. However, his guitar playing does stretch a little further, although it does seem to fall short of his fingers. This doesn't stop him from performing exciting experiments, it just makes it really difficult to see what he's doing, because most of the time he's too afraid to look.

SCIENCE MUSEUM

PUNK SCiENCE

THE Intergalactic, SUPERMASSIVE SPACE BOOK

Written by Jon Milton

Illustrated by Dan Hope

MACMILLAN CHILDREN'S BOOKS

This book is produced in association with the Science Museum. Sales of this book support the Science Museum's exhibitions and programmes.

Internationally recognized as one of the world's leading science centres, the Science Museum, London, contains more than 10,000 amazing exhibits, two fantastic simulator rides and the astounding IMAX cinema. Enter a world of discovery and achievement, where you can see, touch and experience real objects and icons which have shaped the world we live in today or visit www.sciencemuseum.org.uk to find out more.

First published 2014 by Macmillan Children's Books
a division of Macmillan Publishers Limited
20 New Wharf Road, London N1 9RR
Basingstoke and Oxford
Associated companies throughout the world
www.panmacmillan.com

ISBN 978-1-4472-5384-6

1 3 5 7 9 8 6 4 2

A CIP catalogue record for this book is available from the British Library.

Printed and bound by CPI Group (UK) Ltd, Croydon CR0 4YY

Contents

To Mum and Dad

Thanks to Gaby Morgan, Wendy Burford,
Beth Linfield and Dr Harry Cliff

Hello! We're Jon and Dan

from Punk Science, and we spend most of our time at Punk Science HQ perched on the top of the Science Museum in London, surrounded by weird and wonderful objects. While we're up there we do all sorts of exciting experiments, delightful demonstrations and scintillating science shows.

So I suppose you're wondering what this book is about?

It is about space in all it's incredible giganticness.

Before we get on to that we wanted to point out that this book is yours and you'll find facts in it, you can play games and quizzes, you can scribble in it, draw in it, dribble on it . . . actually try not to dribble on it; that will make the paper soggy.

We the Punk Science team will try to guide you through space as best we can but as space is so big it's bigger than the biggest thing ever, there is a chance we might get lost ourselves.

About Jon

Job: Punk Scientist
Location: Science Museum
Favourite Colour: Puce
Favourite Food: Cheese flavour banana
Favourite Astronaut: Helen Sharman
(first Briton in Space)

About Dan

Job: Punk Scientist
Location: Science Museum
Favourite Colour: Cerise
Favourite Food: Deep-fried ice cream
Favourite Astronaut: Valentina Tereshkova
(first woman in Space)

Chapter One

Spaceships and Satellites

We'd better get started by heading off into space . . . but we're going to need some wheels . . . What's that? We can't use the Punk Science van to go into space, we need a spaceship?

What about just a ship?

What do you mean, 'no'? Fine, have it your way. It looks like we'll have to learn a bit about spaceships.

It's time to get on board with Punk Science and set a course for Facts!

First fact of the book, get ready, here goes . . .

Rockets tend to have a pointy end and a fiery end!

Not impressed?

How about this?

Rockets come in many shapes and sizes and they all tend to work by burning fuel which pushes behind the rocket and has a reaction of pushing the rocket forward.

That wasn't so bad, was it? It's not exactly rocket science, is it? Oh, it is and that's meant to be tricky.

And to be honest, it is.

Flying into space is hard: you need lots of power, lots of fuel and once you are in space you need to be able to cope without air being readily available and being in reduced gravity.

Maybe if we have a look at the some of the numerous spacecraft that have journeyed into space we might be able to get up there ourselves.

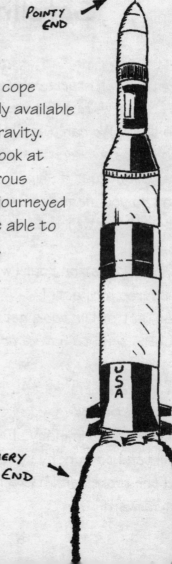

POINTY END

FIERY END

Rocket Facts

We really need to start with the history of rockets, because it was the technology developed from these early rockets that led to rockets going into space:

- The Chinese were using solid-fuel rockets nearly 1,000 years ago.

- In 1804, English inventor William Congreve develops a rocket to be used in battle, not a particularly friendly use for a rocket.

- In 1844, another William, William Hale, comes up with a more accurate spinning rocket that blew things up more accurately, which is even less friendly.

- Jump ahead to 1903. Konstantin Tsiolkovsky had an idea for a much friendlier use for rockets by using them to go into space.

- Rockets used solid fuels until American Robert Goddard thought it might be better to use liquid fuels. His first go at it wasn't very successful as it didn't go very high and landed in a cabbage patch.

- However, in 1926, Goddard did make a liquid-fuelled rocket that went up a whole mile.

- During World War Two (1939–1945) Werner von Braun developed the V-2 rocket. Which again wasn't particularly nice as it was used as a weapon. However, he did later help the USA to develop the rockets that went to space.

The space race

After the end of the Second World War in 1945 a kind of unofficial competition started between the USA and USSR (which is now Russia and quite a few of its neighbouring countries). It was a race for space itself. It was much like the race Dan and I have when there is only one biscuit left but two of us. Actually, it's nothing like that . . . a race for biscuits is much more important.

This is Sputnik 1 and in October 1957 it was the first artificially launched satellite. It was built by the Soviet Union.

It weighed 83.8kg and took 98 minutes to orbit the earth.

Russia got into space first, but the USA made it to the moon first, so we'll call it a draw. Here are some of the important dates to put in your diary . . . if you have a historical diary . . . which you probably don't, and frankly it'd be odd if you did.

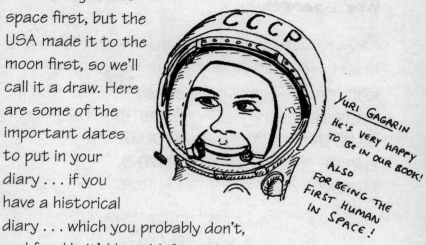

YURI GAGARIN
HE'S VERY HAPPY
TO BE IN OUR BOOK!
ALSO
FOR BEING THE
FIRST HUMAN
IN SPACE!

- 1957 Russia lauched Sputnik 1 and put the first animal in space, a dog called Laika. The Americans dubbed her 'Muttnik'.

- 1961 Russians put the first human in space; he was called Yuri Gagarin.

- 1969 US astronauts Neil Armstrong and Buzz Aldrin land on the moon.

- 1981 The US launches the first Space Shuttle mission.

- 2000 First crew arrive on the International Space Station. It's been continually inhabited ever since. People from lots of nations including USA and Russia all happily work together on the ISS.

Word search

Can you find these words hidden in the grid? They may be horizontal, vertical, diagonal or even backwards.

ROCKET

SHUTTLE

SATELLITE

ENGINE

MODULE

BLAST

BOOSTER

APOLLO

SPUTNIK

LAUNCH

There is also a word in there that has nothing to do with space at all but can you find it?

R	Q	B	L	S	A	T	E	L	L	I	T	E	J	P
O	G	H	W	Z	C	V	T	Y	U	D	C	X	M	M
C	N	P	O	G	B	E	A	A	K	H	A	B	W	O
K	L	F	S	A	E	W	Z	J	O	V	P	O	P	D
E	R	E	B	O	O	S	T	E	R	W	O	Q	M	U
T	M	N	B	V	K	S	D	D	E	X	L	Z	P	L
F	G	S	H	U	T	T	L	E	E	W	L	K	L	E
H	S	A	A	V	B	M	N	D	T	Y	O	U	I	P
T	Y	U	F	J	F	D	J	D	N	K	O	P	O	L
J	R	K	P	L	T	Y	C	N	X	B	A	S	D	E
H	C	N	U	A	L	H	V	B	C	X	L	I	O	P
P	O	I	U	Y	T	R	E	W	A	S	S	A	F	G
J	K	V	K	I	N	T	U	P	S	C	X	Z	S	B
V	V	S	K	A	T	E	B	O	A	R	D	D	D	T
L	E	N	G	I	N	E	K	J	H	G	F	D	S	A

Answers on page 85

Spaceship Facts

We made a Punk Science spaceship – it was one metre high, which was a bit of a miscalculation as it was too small for us to get in it.

Here's how big proper spaceships are:

Russian R7 = 29 metres

European Ariane 5 = 51 metres

USA Space Shuttle = 55.4 metres

Russian Proton = 60 metres

USA Titan = 65 metres

USA Saturn V = a whopping 110 metres

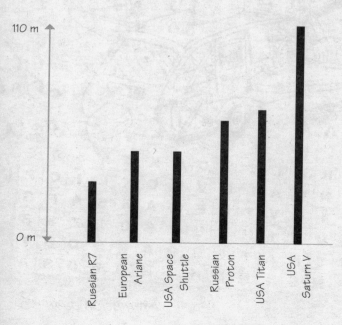

Space maze

Navigation is important. See if you can navigate the Punk Science spaceship through the asteroid field.

Answer on page 85

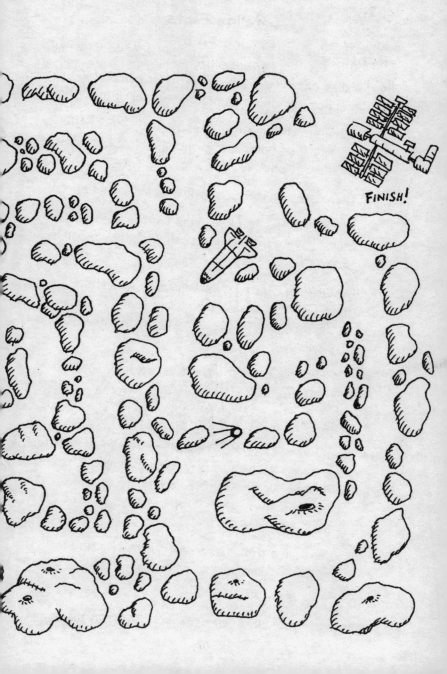

FINISH!

Satellite Facts

Ever thought about what a satellite does?

- Well, a satellite is something that orbits objects in space such as a planet like earth.

- Some satellites are for astronomy, some monitor the weather, some are for communication, some for navigation and some are for spying.

- There are about 2,500 satellites orbiting earth.

- They don't have to be things that humans have built either. For example, technically the moon is a satellite.

- We've seen Sputnik 1 earlier, which was the first artificial satellite, but the first American artificial satellite, launched in 1958, was called Explorer 1.

- There are even satellites that orbits other planets like Mars.

- The earth itself is a satellite of the sun.

- Satellites that stay in orbit at one fixed position are called 'geostationary'. Geostationary means the satellite orbits in the same direction and at the same speed as the earth spins, so it stays above the same spot.

- A satellite that has a polar orbit travels around the earth from pole to pole.

Here are five more facts for you to fill the space in your head with!

- The American lunar lander that first landed on the moon was called 'Eagle'.

- The Saturn V was the rocket that took the Apollo missions to the moon.

- The J-2 was the name of the engine that was used on the Saturn V rockets.

- On the Apollo 17 mission astronauts spent 75 hours on the moon.

- In 1971 Apollo 15 put the first car on the moon . . . well, the first lunar rover, to give it its proper name.

Space Shuttle Facts

The Space Shuttle was the first spaceship that could return to earth and be reused.

- Space Shuttles could carry 26,786kg, which is about the same as four African elephants.

- The first Space Shuttle was launched in 1981 and was called Columbia.

- The Discovery Space Shuttle has flown more missions than any other spacecraft.

- The last Shuttle mission was on 21 July 2011.

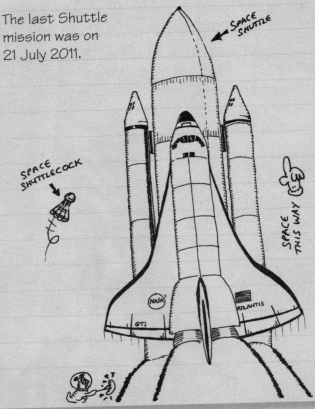

SPACE SHUTTLE

SPACE SHUTTLECOCK

SPACE THIS WAY

Spot the difference

Can you spot and circle eight differences between these two pictures?

Answers on page 86

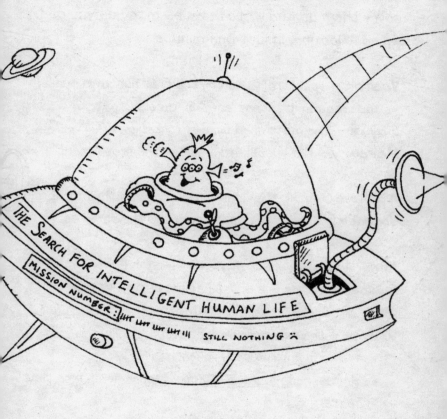

Memory test

Look at this list of names of spaceships and
satellites. Go on: have a really good look! Now
cover them up and write down as many as you can,
without looking, in just one minute.

Vostok — spacecraft used by the first human in space,
   Yuri Gagarin. It means 'east' in Russian.

Soyuz — the most used type of rocket ever.

Mercury — the spacecraft used by the first American in
   space.

Apollo — 6 Apollo missions put humans on the moon.

Voyager — spacecraft sent to explore the outer solar
   system.

Mir — a Russian space station.

Spaceship One — a private space plane designed to
   take tourists into space.

Gemini — the name of missions before Apollo that
   tested out docking techniques, dealing with
   weightlessness and the effects of spending a long time
   in space.

International Space Station — launched in 1998,
   it's the largest artificial object in space.

Endeavour — Space Shuttle first launched in 1992.

Atlantis — another Space Shuttle, but this was first
   launched in 1985.

Crossword

Across

1. An object, planet or moon that orbits something else.
5. The first vehicle used to land on the moon.
6. When a rocket takes off.
7. Sir Isaac had three laws of this.
8. A European spacecraft.
9. A type of spacecraft

Down

1. A reusable space vehicle.
2. A rocket and the name of a moon.
3. Sir Isaac's last name.
4. The first satellite in space.
7. Name of a rocket and a planet.

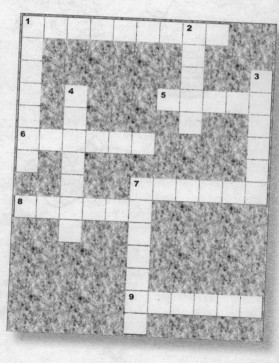

Answers on page 86

Mini-rocket experiment

For this experiment you will need:

1 empty film canister
some effervescent tablets
(they fizz in water: ask a grown-up for these)
and some water.

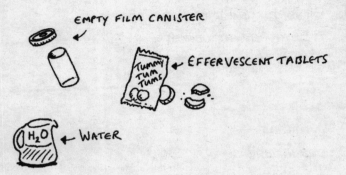

Put some water into the canister and

place half the tablet on the lid of the film canister.

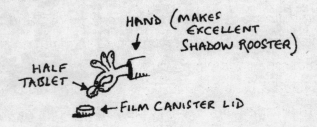

Now all you need to do is put the lid on,

give it a shake, place it lid down on the table and stand back!

SHAKE IT!

Make sure you stand back as they might go pop in your face, which would be bad for your face.

Inside the rocket little bubbles of carbon dioxide are fizzing.

Eventually there is so much carbon dioxide in the canister it starts squashing the water. But there is only so much squashing the water can take until it finally says, 'That's it! I'm leaving,' and with a big build-up of pressure the lid pops off, and the canister flies off into space or, failing that, a couple of metres in the air. If you want to get into space you need a pretty big rocket, with some pretty big fuel tanks. But that is just to get out of the earth's atmosphere. If we launched rockets from the moon, we wouldn't need so much power or fuel because the force of gravity is much less there. (You still need to get to the moon in the first place though!)

All this helps to show us Sir Isaac Newton's Third Law of Motion which states that 'For every action there is an equal and opposite reaction'.

In our rockets the force of the pop pushes the lid and contents out of the canister.

That's the action.

The reaction is when the rocket goes in the opposite direction, up into the air.

It's like swimming. When you do breaststroke you push the water back, but what happens? You move forward. The same thing happens with the rocket.

Space jokes

Space travel is no laughing matter . . . except on this page where it is.

What's the most popular game in space?
Astro-nauts and crosses

Did you hear the one about the spaceship?
It was out of this world

Why can't astronauts type?
Because they keep pressing the space bar

What is an astronaut's favourite salad?
Rocket

How does an astronaut get a baby to sleep?
Rock-it

Why are false teeth like stars?
Because they both come out at night

25

Spacecraft Fuel Facts

Early rockets used gunpowder (solid fuel). More modern rockets tend to use hydrogen or kerosene (liquid fuel). The Space Shuttles actually used both.

We experimented with a liquid-fart-based rocket fuel, the results of which are too disgusting ever to mention. Here's a look at some alternatives to conventional rocket fuel.

Here are some other ways spacecraft can propel themselves . . .

Solar sails

There are plans for spaceships that will be powered by big sails that use the pressure of sunlight, but they aren't for space pirates. The acceleration starts off pretty low, so they can't carry humans yet. But they can accelerate to speeds of around 90 km per second. At that speed they could travel from London to New York in just over a minute; that's over ten times faster than

← SPACE ANCHOR

S.S. PUNK SCIENCE

* BAD ARTIST'S IMPRESSION

the Space Shuttle was. They should be up and running in the next ten years . . .

Ion engines

Ion engines work by electrically charging a gas (usually xenon) so that it releases ions. An ion is an atom or molecule that is electrically charged.

The ions are released from the back of the engine, pushing the spacecraft forward.

A modern ion-powered spacecraft can go up to 90,000 metres a second.

And, yes, it's ions not irons.

Nuclear-powered spaceships

Rockets run by nuclear fission are more fuel-efficient, and so much lighter, than chemical rockets. This means that nuclear spaceships could travel twice as fast as our current chemical spacecraft.

The main problem with nuclear-fission engines is that they might be dangerous for the astronauts so it might be necessary to use robots instead.

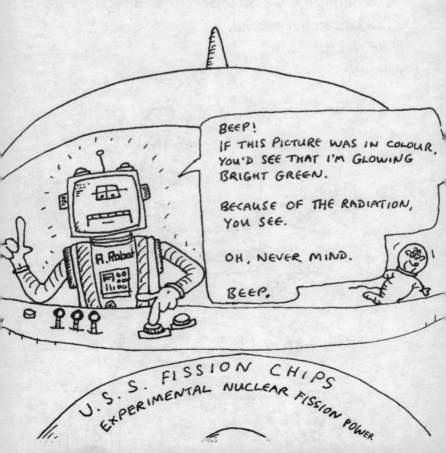

Teleportation

Why don't we just teleport ourselves to other planets? Well, perhaps we could one day, since scientists have managed to teleport a photon (a tiny bit of light), but teleporting a human is probably impossible. There is also the added problem that when you teleport, an exact copy of you would be made, but unfortunately the original would be destroyed. So the 'you' isn't you: it's a copy without the bits that make you you. So, no good for you but OK for the 'new you', that's not you. Wow, that is complicated.

BIG Qs

Time to test your brains with these tricky questions. Remember: no cheating! Circle the correct answer.

1. How much did Sputnik 1 weigh?
   a. 145.2 tons
   b. 83.8 kg
   c. The same as 10 elephants with big shoes on

2. How long did it take Sputnik 1 to orbit the earth?
   a. 98 minutes
   b. 2 days
   c. 6 minutes 35 seconds

3. What was the name of the lunar lander that was the first to touch down on the moon?
   a. Hawk
   b. Parrot
   c. Eagle

4. Name the 3 astronauts on the Apollo 11 mission.
   a. Armstrong, Aldrin, Collins
   b. Armstrong, Aldrin, Lovell
   c. Armstrong, Stafford, Cernan

5. What is a satellite?
   a.   Something that orbits planets or other objects in space
   b.   Something that helps you watch TV
   c.   A bit like a Satel only lighter

6. Is the moon a satellite?
   a.   No
   b.   Yes
   c.   Maybe, who's asking?

7. Approximately how many satellites are in orbit around the earth?
   a.   8
   b.   8 million
   c.   8,000

8. When talking about satellites, what does 'geostationary' mean?
   a.   Paper and pens that belong to someone called Geo
   b.   A type of orbit 35,786 km above the earth where satellites stay in a fixed position
   c.   A type of orbit with lots of movement all over the place

9. What was the first American artificial satellite called?
   a. Exploder 1
   b. Explorer 1
   c. Eggs-sandwich 1

10. Solid-fuel rockets were first used by the Chinese, but when?
   a. nearly 100 years ago
   b. nearly 1,000 years ago
   c. nearly 10,000 years ago

11. The first liquid-fuelled rocket was built by American Robert Goddard in 1926, but where did it land after its maiden voyage?
   a. In a dustbin
   b. On a cabbage patch
   c. On a roof

12. What was the name of the first Space Shuttle launched in 1981?
   a. Insomnia
   b. Columbia
   c. Clive

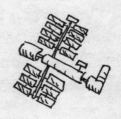

13. How much stuff could the Space Shuttle hold?

    a.   26,786 kg

    b.   86 kg

    c.   2 bags of sugar, a bow tie, a small badger and a ball of fluff

14. Which single spacecraft has flown the most missions?

    a.   The Discovery Space Shuttle

    b.   The Discovery Rocket

    c.   The Disco Ship

15. The Hubble space telescope which is used to look to the far reaches of our universe was deployed in which year?

    a.   1895

    b.   2001

    c.   1990

Answers on page 87

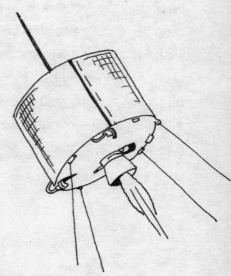

Chapter Two

Astronauts
Discover what people need to live in space

Astronauts are the people (and sometimes animals) that travel into space. But they aren't always called astronauts: they have other names — and we don't mean their actual names, like Barbara and Kevin. Anyway you'll find out more about that later.

We Punk Scientists would love to be astronauts. However, there are a couple of things holding us back. Firstly, you have to be intelligent, also brave, also physically fit, also be able to count to 20 without taking your socks off. These are all things that aren't really our thing. But as you're probably all those things, you shouldn't have any problem at all being an astronaut. To help you out this chapter has a few astronauty facts.

Word search

Can you find these words in the grid? They may be horizontal, vertical or diagonal.

HELMET

BOOTS

GLOVES

COSMONAUT

SPACESUIT

ARMSTRONG

GAGARIN

ASTRONAUT

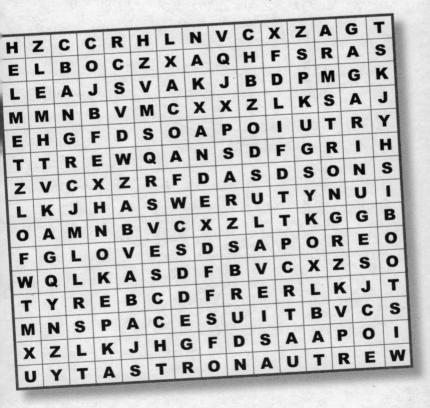

H	Z	C	C	R	H	L	N	V	C	X	Z	A	G	T
E	L	B	O	C	Z	X	A	Q	H	F	S	R	A	S
L	E	A	J	S	V	A	K	J	B	D	P	M	G	K
M	M	N	B	V	M	C	X	X	Z	L	K	S	A	J
E	H	G	F	D	S	O	A	P	O	I	U	T	R	Y
T	T	R	E	W	Q	A	N	S	D	F	G	R	I	H
Z	V	C	X	Z	R	F	D	A	S	D	S	O	N	S
L	K	J	H	A	S	W	E	R	U	T	Y	N	U	I
O	A	M	N	B	V	C	X	Z	L	T	K	G	G	B
F	G	L	O	V	E	S	D	S	A	P	O	R	E	O
W	Q	L	K	A	S	D	F	B	V	C	X	Z	S	O
T	Y	R	E	B	C	D	F	R	E	R	L	K	J	T
M	N	S	P	A	C	E	S	U	I	T	B	V	C	S
X	Z	L	K	J	H	G	F	D	S	A	A	P	O	I
U	Y	T	A	S	T	R	O	N	A	U	T	R	E	W

Answers on page 87

35

Spot the difference

Can you spot and circle nine differences between these two pictures?

Answers on page 87

Astronaut Facts

- Astronauts aren't just called astronauts. In Russia they are known as cosmonauts and in China they are called taikonauts.

- Astronaut comes from the Greek words 'astron' which means star and 'nautes' which means sailor, so there are actually star sailors.

- With Cosmonaut we again have 'naut' at the end meaning sailor but this time the 'cosmo' bit means universe, so the Russians have universe sailors.

- And finally in China, we have space sailors because 'taiko' comes from the Chinese for space.

- At least they all agree they are sailors of some sort – not that they actually do any sailing. Unless of course they use a spaceship with solar sails like we saw earlier.

- However, all these terms refer to professional space travellers. If you are one of the increasing number of space tourists you are officially known as a 'spaceflight participant' which is a rubbish name. We think they should be renamed as super-mega-astro-cosmo-traveller-nauts, but as it's not very catchy we don't expect it will catch on.

What does an astronaut use this for?

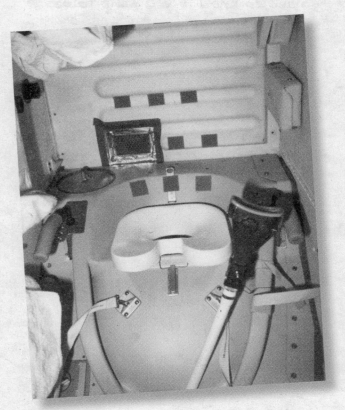

Clues:

- A seat with a hole in
- A seat belt
- A funnel . . . hmmmm

Answer on page 88

Here are some facts you really need to know if you want to be an astronaut

- You can get space sickness, which is a bit like sea sickness.

Nearly everything in space is dry. Well, not everything: water is still wet. Because of the lack of rivers and reservoirs in space, water has to be rationed, which means . . .

- Dry toilets. There is no flush, just a vacuum to suck the poo away.

- Dry shampoo. Oh yes, you can wash your hair without water. Or if you're Dan you can just not wash it at all.

- Dry food . . . not all the time. Water is often added to make it edible: otherwise imagine how dry your mouth would get eating it.

You're taller in space because gravity is not as strong as it is on earth.

You have to be strapped down while you sleep otherwise you'd just float about.

The good news is that nothing gets covered in dust because it never settles. The bad news is that there still is dust — it's just floating everywhere.

Thought scientific experiments could only be done on earth? You thought wrong! Astronauts do a lot of experiments on the ISS.

Astronauts did experiments to show if frogs could jump in space and found out that they couldn't. Instead the frogs just kind of somersaulted around and around and around.

They also did experiments to see if birds could fly in space. They couldn't. Instead they just did loop-the-loops, hopefully avoiding the somersaulting frogs.

Apollo capsule

This is the Apollo 10 capsule which you can see at the Science Museum. It's been into space and back. But how many people do you think could fit in this tiny little capsule?

A.   10

B.   3

C.   1

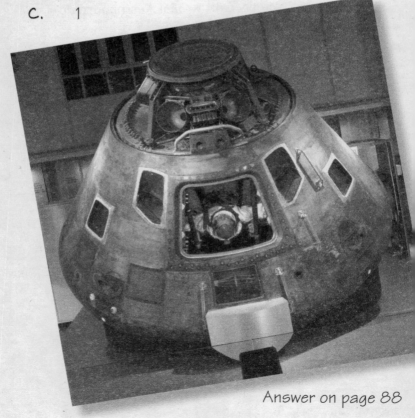

Answer on page 88

Crossword

Across

1. The first dog in space
4. First name of astronaut Grissom
6. Russian 'universe sailor'
8. First name of the first person on the moon
9. American 'star sailor'
10. Last name of the first Briton in space

Down

2. Last name of the first person on the moon
3. Something you need to wear on your head in space
4. Last name of the first person in space
5. Something you need to wear on the rest of you in space
7. First name of the first woman in space

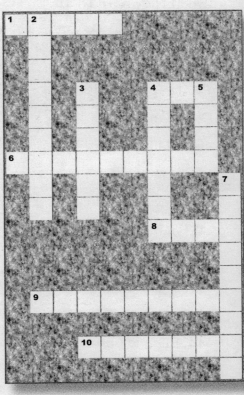

Answers on page 88

43

Moon People

Not many people have been on the moon, and to be honest it was quite a long time ago when they were. We think it's about time to go back and set up Punk Science Moonbase HQ. What do you think? What do you mean, we couldn't? Oh, because we're idiots. Yeah, good point!

Here is a list of who has been on the moon and when they were there.

1.	Neil Armstrong	Apollo 11, 21 July 1969
2.	Buzz Aldrin	Apollo 11, 21 July 1969
3.	Pete Conrad	Apollo 12, 19 Nov 1969
4.	Alan Bean	Apollo 12, 19 Nov 1969
5.	Alan Shepard	Apollo 14, 5 Feb 1971
6.	Edgar Mitchell	Apollo 14, 5 Feb 1971
7.	David Scott	Apollo 15, 30 July 1971
8.	James Irwin	Apollo 15, 30 July 1971
9.	John W. Young	Apollo 16, 21 April 1972
10.	Charles Duke	Apollo 16, 21 April 1972
11.	Harrison Schmitt	Apollo 17, 11 Dec 1972
12.	Eugene Cernan	Apollo 17, 11 Dec 1972

Extra Astro-Facts

- They were all American and men. Could you be the first woman on the moon?

- Humans haven't been back to the moon since 1972, which is quite a long time. Perhaps you could get to work at being the next person on the moon.

- The youngest person on the moon was Charles Duke, who was 36 at the time.

- The oldest person on the moon was Alan Shepard, who was 47 at the time.

- When Neil Armstrong first set foot on the moon, he famously said, 'This is one small step for man, one giant leap for mankind.' Which sounds very impressive, unless you know the truth, which is he fluffed his lines. He should have said, 'This is one small step for a man . . .' This makes a bit more sense when you think about it.

- Which foot did Neil Armstrong use to step on the moon?
  His left.

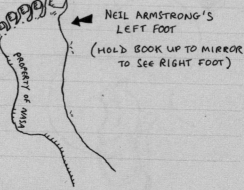

NEIL ARMSTRONG'S LEFT FOOT

(HOLD BOOK UP TO MIRROR TO SEE RIGHT FOOT)

PROPERTY OF NASA

Space connections

Follow the ropes to find out which two astronauts are connected.

Answer on page 88

Astro-nauts and crosses

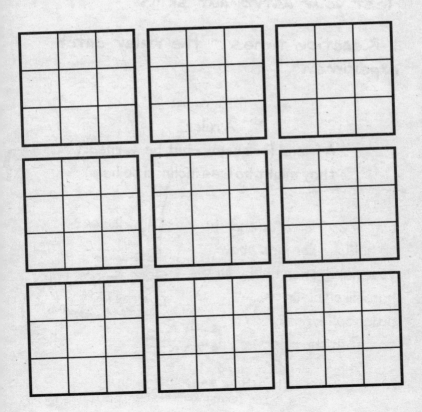

On a long journey into space you'll need something to keep you occupied. How about a nice game of astro-nauts and crosses? It's easy to play: just take turns with a friend or enemy to put a nought or a cross in the grids below. The winner is whoever gets a vertical, horizontal or diagonal line of three all the way across.

Welcome to Punk Science Astronaut Training

To be an astronaut you need to have quite a lot of talents. Being a really good pilot can help, or a really good scientist. But you also need to be fit in your body and brain, so here are some exercises to help you.

Test your astronaut skills

1. Reaction times — the ruler catch experiment

You'll need:

A ruler

A friend (or enemy —but be warned: they might be less inclined to help)

Get your friend (or enemy) to hold a ruler just above your hand, then hold your hand like this in order to be ready to catch the ruler.

RULER

YOUR FRIEND'S (OR ENEMY'S) HAND

YOUR HAND (EXACT REPRESENTATION)

Get your friend (or enemy) to drop the ruler — but the trick is that they must take you by surprise and not tell you that they are going to drop it before they do so.

At first, if you catch the ruler at about the halfway mark you're doing well, but you'll need to react quicker if you want to be an astronaut: so practise until you catch the ruler with just a couple of centimetres of the ruler in your hand!

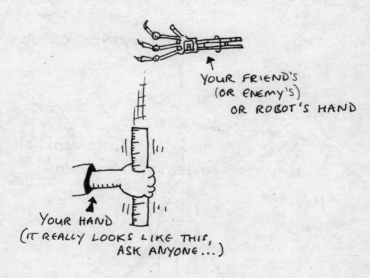

YOUR FRIEND'S
(OR ENEMY'S)
OR ROBOT'S HAND

YOUR HAND
(IT REALLY LOOKS LIKE THIS,
ASK ANYONE...)

If you like, you could swap around and give your friend a go, but don't swap with your enemy as they'll only use their new fast reactions for evil.

2. Flying skills – circle the correct place to land

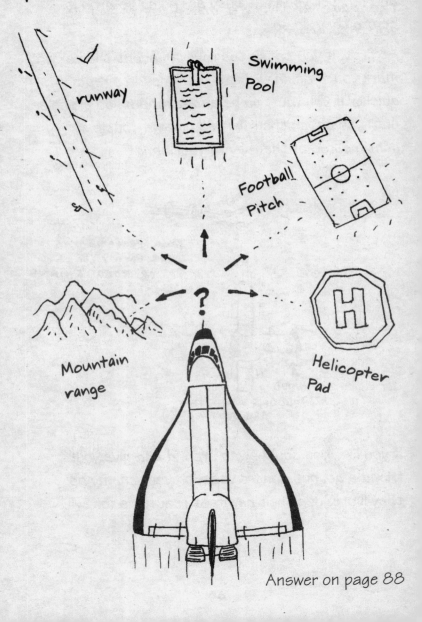

runway

Swimming Pool

Football Pitch

Mountain range

Helicopter Pad

Answer on page 88

3. Memory test — look at these objects for a minute and then cover the page and write down as many as you can remember.

STOPWATCH

NOVELTY SINGING FISH

JON'S FAVOURITE SOCK

KETTLE (FOR MAKING DAN A CUP OF TEA)

CUPCAKE

BROKEN TENNIS RACKET

DAN'S CUP OF TEA

DAN'S BASS GUITAR

BANANA SKIN

JON'S PENCIL AND NOTEPAD

THAT ONE YOU ALWAYS FORGET... HMMM... WHAT IS IT?

SMALL FROG

Quiztro-nauts

Here's your chance to see how much you know about space travellers.

1. What is the number of the Apollo capsule in the Science Museum? _____

2. Which animal jumped around in circles while in space?_____

3. What are Chinese Astronauts known as? _____

4. Where would you be taller – on earth or in space?_____

5. In what year did the last person go to the moon? _____

6. What was the name of the first dog in space?_____

7. In what year did the first man go into space?_____

8. What was the name of the first woman in space?_____

Answers on page 89

More space jokes

Did you hear about the two astronauts that did ten space missions back to back?
They didn't like looking at each other

Why do astronauts have the best parties?
Because they are out of this world

What did the comet say to the other comet?
Pleased to meteor

What's the centre of gravity?
V

Which astronaut wears the biggest helmet?
The one with the biggest head

Which is the most musical planet?
Nep-tune

Chapter Three

The Solar System
A look at planet earth and its neighbours

Do you know where you live? Really? Are you sure? We don't mean your house and your street, not even the town you live in or even the country. Punk Science likes to think about things on a bigger scale. We're talking about the solar system you live in, which *we* like to think of as a bit like your street, in terms of the whole universe, and a pretty small street it would be too.

The Solar System is the part of space we live in. It's made up of the sun and planets and lots of other stuff that you'll find out more about later on.

The sun is the centre of the Solar System.

It's over 4 billion years old, which is slightly older than your gran (not strictly true).

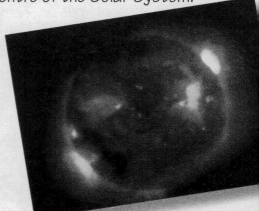

Its surface temperature is

5,500 degrees Celsius, which is hot, but not as hot as the core which is 15 million degrees Celsius, which is hotter than the hottest thing

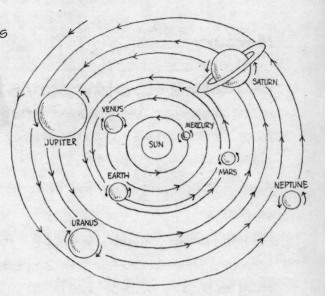

you can think of . . . unless of course you're thinking of the sun: then it's pretty much exactly the same level of hotness.

The sun is also very big; you could get about a million planet earths inside it.

That is, if there weren't loads of nuclear reactions going on in the sun's core. It is these nuclear reactions that provide the sun's energy. There are nuclear reactions because the sun is huge and that means that there is a huge amount of gravity at its centre. So much gravity, in fact, that hydrogen atoms are squashed together so hard that they fuse. This fusion energy is what powers the sun, and therefore nearly everything on earth.

Mercury

Mercury is closest to the sun, so it's a bit like the sun's best friend in that respect. It's 57 million km from the sun and it's the smallest planet in the solar system.

A year on Mercury is equivalent to about 88 days on earth.

So good news: you get a lot more birthdays on Mercury. The bad news is the temperature ranges from as high as 430 Celsius or as low as minus 170 Celsius.

Venus

Venus is the planet second closest to the sun. It spins in the opposite direction to the earth, which has got to be weird, right?

A Venus year lasts 224.7 earth days.

And one day on Venus lasts 117 earth days.

It's a bit smaller than earth and is rocky with lots of volcanoes and 464 degrees as its average temperature.

Earth

We can't be bothered telling you about the earth: just look out the window.

But we will tell you about our moon.

The moon is 3,476 km in diameter.

It's about 384,000 km away from you right now and you can still see it at night.

And the big craters you can see are from when it's been hit by asteroids and comets.

Nearly 400 kg of moon rock has been brought back to earth.

The moon would be an ideal place to launch spacecraft from to explore further into the galaxy. The reason is because the force of gravity is weaker on the moon than it is on earth: you wouldn't use as much fuel to launch it, which means you have more fuel for your journey and can go a bit further.

Mars

Not the chocolate bar, the planet.

Fourth closest to the sun.

Called the red planet, because it looks red. Pretty obvious really.

A year on Mars is equivalent to 687 earth days.

A day is 24.63 hours, so quite similar to earth.

The average temperature is minus 63 degrees Celsius. So, not really shorts weather.

Jupiter

Jupiter is the fifth planet from the sun and is unlike the other planets we've seen as it's made of gas, hydrogen and helium.

Its diameter is 142,984 km but it shrinks 2 cm a year, so depending when you're reading this it could be 142,983 km and 99,998 cm by now.

A Jupiter year is equivalent to 11.87 earth years, so not good for having birthdays . . . but good if you want to age slower by having fewer birthdays.

The average temperature is minus 145 degrees Celsius.

Saturn

The one with the rings, which were discovered by Christiaan Huygens. According to NASA it has seven rings.

The rings are made of ice and rock orbiting the planet.

It's the sixth planet from the sun.

A day on Saturn lasts ten and three quarter hours.

A year on Saturn lasts 29.7 earth years.

Uranus

Try saying it out loud without sniggering. Tricky, isn't it?

A year on Uranus lasts 84 earth years and a day lasts 17.24 earth hours.

Like Venus it spins in a clockwise direction.

Its average temperature is about the same as liquid nitrogen, at minus 197 degrees Celsius

It has 27 moons. Here are the names of just a few . . .

Have a good look at them for a minute, then cover them over and write down as many as you can.

Cordelia	Belinda
Ophelia	Perdita
Bianca	Puck
Cressida	Mab
Desdemona	Miranda
Juliet	Ariel
Portia	Umbriel
Rosalind	Titania
Cupid	Oberon

How did you get on?

Neptune

Neptune is an enormous storm of gas.

It looks blue because of all the methane gas in the atmosphere.

It was discovered by Johann Galle in 1846, after its position was predicted by Urbain Le Verrier.

A year on Neptune lasts 164.8 years on earth, and a day lasts just 16.11 hours.

It's a really cold minus 200 degrees Celsius on Neptune as it's the furthest planet away from the sun.

Pluto

Poor old Pluto! It used to be thought of as the ninth planet, but after much consideration it was relegated down to a dwarf planet. Quite right too, as it's actually smaller than our moon, so has no right going around calling itself a planet.

Stars

Stars, like the sun, give off light. They're just really big, nuclear-powered balls of gas. Planets can be made of gas too, but they don't give off light, they just reflect it.

Moons

A moon is a natural satellite that orbits planets. Many planets have more than one moon.

Comets

They're made up of dust and snow, like a messy bedroom in the Arctic. Actually, nothing like a messy bedroom in the Arctic at all. They orbit the sun, and when they get close to it we see comets as bright white streaks in the night sky.

Meteors

Are meteors rocks or dust? Can you guess? They're both! We see them burning up in our atmosphere and are what people think of as 'shooting stars'. But you know otherwise, and can tell those people how incredibly silly they are, and how they are actually meteors.

Meteorites

They sound like meteors but they aren't. They *don't* burn up in our atmosphere and therefore they reach the earth's surface.

Word search

Can you find these planets hidden in the grid? They might be horizontal or vertical.

MERCURY
VENUS
EARTH
MARS
JUPITER
SATURN
URANUS
NEPTUNE

Q	E	T	X	U	O	A	F	M
G	J	G	D	Y	H	Y	F	A
F	V	E	N	U	S	I	S	R
P	M	E	R	C	U	R	Y	S
D	W	Y	F	Q	A	E	J	M
B	J	U	P	I	T	E	R	O
U	T	E	Q	N	V	X	K	H
F	S	Q	E	T	Y	N	P	L
K	H	G	F	D	S	E	L	S
N	B	V	C	X	Z	P	K	A
E	A	R	T	H	G	T	J	T
X	I	Y	D	C	F	U	R	U
V	H	V	C	X	P	N	I	R
Y	T	R	E	W	Q	E	Z	N
C	U	R	A	N	U	S	D	A
R	T	Y	U	I	O	Y	T	E

Answers on page 89

Crossword

Across

2. Planet second closest to the sun
5. The star in our solar system
6. The planet you're on
8. The planet closest to the sun
9. A planet with 27 moons

Down

1. Like a meteor but makes it through the atmosphere
3. Famous for its rings
4. Fifth planet from the sun
7. A natural satellite
8. The red planet

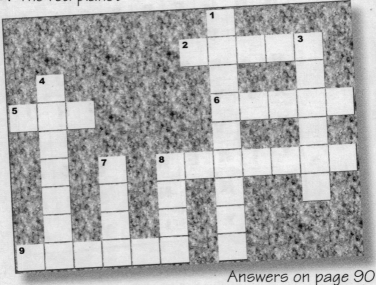

Answers on page 90

Solar System Quiz

1. What is the closest planet to the sun?_____

2. What is the name of the planet furthest away from the sun?_____

3. What is the hottest planet in our solar system?_____

4. What planet is famous for the big red spot on it?_____

5. What planet is famous for the beautiful rings that surround it?_____

6. Can humans breathe as normally in space as they can on earth?_____

7. Is the sun a star or a planet?_____

8. Who was the first person to walk on the moon?_____

9. What planet is known as the red planet?_____

10. What is the name of the force holding us to the earth?_____

Answers on page 90

Chapter Four

The Universe
Black holes, the Big Bang and alien life forms

The universe

If you thought the Solar System was big, you are in for a shock. Because we're now going to explore the universe — which is more enormous than enormous. Which means it's super-amazingly big. We've tried to think about how big it is for a while, which compared with the smallness of our brains (even when combined) is too much to take in. But you can give it a go if you like?

But first the big news: the universe is actually getting bigger!

The universe is expanding, but not because it's eaten too much food: it's because of the Big Bang.

The Big Bang happened nearly 14 billion years ago and created everything in the universe, all space, all matter, and even time itself.

What's the universe expanding into and what was around before the Big Bang . . . ? Errr, we don't know exactly, which is quite exciting! Maybe *you* could work it out. If you *do*, let us know. Write to Punk Science, Punk Science HQ, Science Museum, Exhibition Road, South Kensington, London. We might steal your ideas and pretend *we* had them though . . . just warning you.

Stars

The closest star to us apart from the sun (which is about 150 million km away) is Proxima Centauri. This is so far away we're going to measure it in something called 'light years'.

A light year is a measurement of distance like a metre or a kilometre. It's much longer than a metre or a kilometre though. It's the distance light travels in a year — and that is 9.5 trillion km. So, Proxima Centauri is 4.22 light years away or 40,000,000,000,000 km. (It's a really long way.)

When we see stars from earth we tend to recognize them through the constellations. Constellation are patterns or shapes that we see the stars forming in the night sky. They are usually named after figures from mythology or signs of the zodiac, like Virgo or Pisces. The thing is, although they look close together to us here on earth, the stars that make up constellations aren't actually very close to each other at all, and are in fact many light years apart.

The Milky Way

Our galaxy is called the Milky Way. It's made up of hundreds of billions of stars, and there are many other galaxies in the universe. The furthest galaxies we can see are 30 billion light years away.

Black holes

'Black holes' are stars that have collapsed — not on the sofa because they are tired type of collapsing: a much, *much* bigger type of collapsing.

They'd be the ultimate at intergalactic hide and seek because they're tricky to spot as they don't give off any light. But we can work out where they are because they have a really powerful gravitational pull that pulls in gas from nearby stars and it's this we can see.

Don't, whatever you do, dip your toe in one as, once you are in a black hole, gravity is so strong there is no way of getting out again.

If you see something go into a black hole, it will appear stretched by the force of gravity and look like a thin strand of spaghetti which is called 'spaghettification'. You might say you're pasta the point of no return. (Or you might not.)

Join the dots

Join the dots to form some constellations.

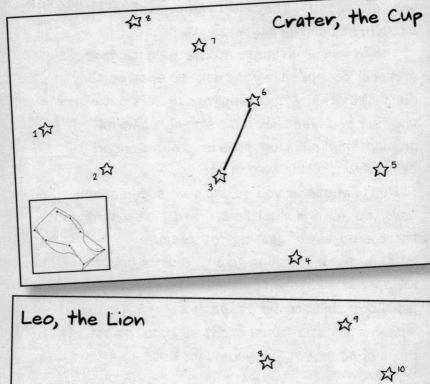

Crater, the Cup

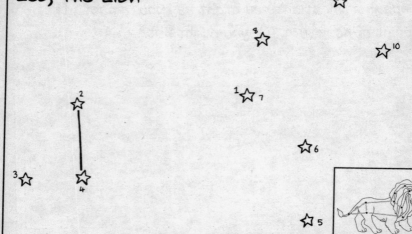

Leo, the Lion

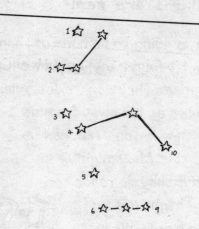

Orion, the Hunter

1 ☆ ☆
2 ☆—☆

3 ☆   ☆
4 ☆

☆
☆
☆ 11
☆ 12
☆ 13
☆ 14

☆ 10

5 ☆

6 ☆—☆—☆ 9

7 ☆   ☆ 8

scorpius, the Scorpion

☆ ☆
☆ ☆ ☆ ☆ ☆ 14
10 11 12 13

☆ 9   ☆ 15

☆ 16

1 ☆   ☆ 8

2 ☆
3 ☆   ☆ 7

4 ☆

5 ☆   6 ☆

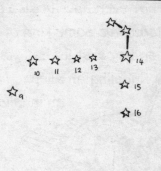

71

Which of these aliens are real?

The answer is going to be none of them, as we haven't found any yet, but that doesn't mean they don't exist. Aliens could live so far away from us that they haven't reached us yet . . . but they might.

And if they do reach us they might not be little and green with big heads. We just don't know how evolution could have worked on other planets. They could have no skeletons, they could be really tiny or really big, they may not even have bodies at all, and could be some kind of intelligent gas. Yes, a gas: so be careful what you breathe as you might be inhaling an alien . . .

an inhalien.

Gravity drop

Newton wasn't the first person to think about gravity. The sixteenth century Italian scientist Galileo performed a really simple experiment that you can try right now. Well, not right now . . . you'll need to read how to do it first.

Galileo used cannon balls for this, but we couldn't find any, and even if we could we're all too weedy to pick them up.

So take a piece of paper and a tennis ball.

Scrunch up the piece of paper so it's about the same size as the ball. Now hold them up and drop them.

Despite the obvious weight difference, they'll both hit the ground at almost the same time.

This is because no matter how heavy something is, gravity pulls it down at the same speed.

Find the alien!

Perhaps aliens are good at hiding.
Let's see if you can spot one.

INTERPLANETARY DODGEMS

RAY GUN RANG

MOON ROCK

Answer on page 90

Guess which of these isn't a real constellation

Andromeda – First noted down by Graeco-Roman astronomer Ptolemy. The name comes from Greek mythology. True ☐ False ☐

Boötes – In the northern sky. The name comes from the Greek for 'herdsman' or 'ploughman'. True ☐ False ☐

Cetus – Named after a sea monster in Greek myth. It has 15 main stars in it. True ☐ False ☐

Triangulum Australe – A small constellation in the southern hemisphere. The name is Latin for 'southern triangle'. True ☐ False ☐

The Lawnmower – In the northern hemisphere, just above the grass constellation. True ☐ False ☐

Volans – Represents a flying fish. True ☐ False ☐

Sculptor – Named by Nicolas Louis de Lacaille in the 18th century. It's meant to look like a sculptor. True ☐ False ☐

Reticulum – Latin for 'small net'; it's a small constellation in the southern sky. True ☐ False ☐

Answer on page 90

Five quick facts relating to the universe

1. 13.7 billion years ago the universe begins.

2. Over 4 billion years ago the sun is formed.

3. In 1687 Newton publishes his Three Laws of Motion:

   - 1st law. An object that isn't moving won't start moving unless a force acts upon it.

   - 2nd law. Force is equal to mass times acceleration.

   - 3rd law. Every action has an equal and opposite reaction.

4. In 1916 Einstein publishes his General Theory of Relativity, showing that gravity is formed by the warping of the fabric of space-time. Eh?

5. Light travels at 186,000 miles per second. (Cars travelling on a motorway will travel only about 16 metres in a second. Light is really fast!)

Make your own universe

Making a universe is easy: we do it at Punk Science HQ all the time. In fact we're making one right now. Hang on . . . have we got the words 'universe' and 'ball of snot' confused again? Oh yes, that's exactly what's happened . . . let me just flick it at Dan and we'll get on with making a universe.

You'll need:
A pen
A balloon
Some air to go in the balloon

First blow the balloon up and then deflate it again, being careful not to make a farty noise while you're doing it. We said *not* to make a farty noise.

Now use the pen to mark some dots at random all over the balloon.

Now imagine that the balloon is the entire universe and that the dots are the galaxies. Before you blow up the balloon the galaxies seem pretty close, don't they? But start blowing the balloon up and the universe expands and expands and the galaxies will get further and further apart – and this is just like what's happening to the actual universe.

Gravity Facts

Gravity is the force that gives us weight, because our weight is just a measurement of the effects of gravity on our bodies.

When an apple hit Sir Isaac Newton on the head, he thought, 'I'd better stop sitting around underneath dangerous fruit trees.' He also thought, 'Why do things fall down instead of up?' He went on to think that gravity was the force of attraction between two objects, and that objects that have bigger mass will always pull smaller objects towards them.

The smaller objects will pull a bit themselves but not as much as the bigger object. That's a lot of thinking — which is what you need to do if you are going to write a mathematical theory explaining how gravity behaves.

Gravity pulls us down with less force on the moon because the moon is smaller and has the same density as the earth, so you weigh a sixth of what you would weigh on earth. On other planets the effect of gravity is also different: on Jupiter, for example, you would weigh more than twice what you would weigh on earth, whereas on Mars you'd weigh less than half. But the big one is the sun, where you'd be 270 times heavier than on earth . . . you big lardy.

Einstein vs gravity

Albert Einstein is probably the most famous scientist ever; well, he is at Punk Science HQ anyway.

One of his theories had to do with gravity. It was called the General Theory of Relativity. Yeah, OK, we didn't know what any of that means either, but after we read up about it, we discovered it was about gravity.

ALBERT EINSTEIN

We know that gravity is what keeps our feet on the ground, but it also does a lot more things – and one of those things is that it keeps the earth in orbit around the sun.

Newton wrote about how gravity behaves; Albert Einstein realized how gravity bends space. It sounds pretty difficult to understand, and it is.

We were scratching our heads for weeks until we realized it wasn't the thinking making us scratch our heads: we all actually had a bad case of nits.

Experiment

Here's an experiment to try at home – and all you need is a bed.

Think of all space like your bed.

If you put an object like a football, or a bag filled with books, on top of your bed they would cause dips in the sheet: the heavier the object, the bigger the dip.

These dips pull stuff that's nearby into them. Roll some smaller objects like tennis balls across the bed and you'll see them pulled in by the heavier objects.

Now think of your objects as planets and the bed sheet as the fabric of space-time and that is pretty much how gravity works.

We might know how it works but we are not completely certain why things are attracted to each other. Whoever does come up with the answer will go down in history.

Go on then, start working on it.

HEY!
I'M TRYING TO
SLEEP!

Glossary

Atom the smallest particle of an element, consisting of a nucleus orbited by electrons, that still has the chemical properties of the element.

Celsius a temperature scale named for Anders Celsius in which freezing water is zero and boiling water is 100.

CO2 the symbol for carbon dioxide, a gas which contains one carbon atom and two oxygen atoms.

Density how tightly packed something is.

Diagram a technical drawing, often used to help explain something.

Einstein, Albert the physicist who first theorized that matter and energy are the same thing, and that time and space can mix together.

Electron a sub-atomic particle with a negative electric charge.

Experiment a test or series of tests carried out in order to find answers.

Forces something that exerts a push or pull on an object.

Fusion the process of combining atomic nuclei that releases an enormous amount of energy.

Galileo (1564–1642) an Italian astronomer and physicist.

Gas the state of a substance after a solid and a liquid, where the atoms that make up the substance move around quickly and all over the place.

Gravity the force that pulls all things with a mass towards each other.

Heat a type of energy indicated through temperature.

Helium a type of gas that is lighter than air.

Hydrogen a chemical element that is normally a gas or part of water.

Ice a solid state of water.

Ion an atom or molecule that is electrically charged.

Kerosene a petrol-based type of fuel.

Mass how much of something there is.

Molecules the combination of the elements that make up a compound.

NASA National Aeronautics and Space Administration.

Neutrons particles in the nucleus of an atom.

Nuclear referring to atomic nuclei, as in nuclear energy.

Oxygen an element that is part of the air we breathe.

Particles really tiny pieces of something.

Pressure the exertion of force on something.

Proton a positively charged particle found in the nucleus of an atom.

Reaction a response or force that is equal or opposite to another force.

Relativity according to Galileo, relativity shows that the laws of physics remain the same no matter where you are or how fast you are moving.

Solar sail a theoretical device similar to a wind sail that catches solar radiation to propel a ship. One day solar sail may power a spacecraft.

Space-time a way of describing the universe in which there are four dimensions: three of space and one of time; it is associated with Einstein's theories.

Sun big hot thing in the sky.

Telescope a device that uses lenses to make distant objects appear closer.

Temperature how cold or hot something is.

Weight how heavy something is.

Answers

Page 8. Word search

R	Q	B	L	S	A	T	E	L	L	I	T	E	J	P
O	G	H	W	Z	C	V	T	Y	U	D	C	X	M	M
C	N	P	O	G	B	E	A	A	K	H	A	B	W	O
K	L	F	S	A	E	W	Z	J	O	V	P	O	P	D
E	R	E	B	O	O	S	T	E	R	W	O	Q	M	U
T	M	N	B	V	K	S	D	D	E	X	L	Z	P	L
F	G	S	H	U	T	T	L	E	E	W	L	K	L	E
H	S	A	A	V	B	M	N	D	T	Y	O	U	I	P
T	Y	U	F	J	F	D	J	D	N	K	O	P	O	L
J	R	K	P	L	T	Y	C	N	X	B	A	S	D	E
H	C	N	U	A	L	H	V	B	C	X	L	I	O	P
P	O	I	U	Y	T	R	E	W	A	S	S	A	F	G
J	K	V	K	I	N	T	U	P	S	C	X	Z	S	B
V	V	S	K	A	T	E	B	O	A	R	D	D	D	T
L	E	N	G	I	N	E	K	J	H	G	F	D	S	A

Page 10. Space maze

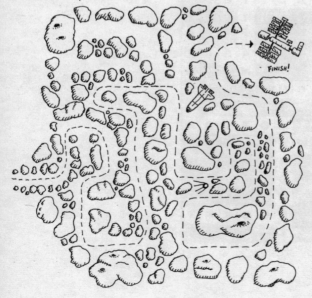

FINISH!

85

Page 16. Spot the difference

Page 19. Crossword

86

Page 30. Big Qs

1. b
2. a
3. c
4. a
5. a
6. b
7. c
8. b
9. b
10. b
11. b
12. b
13. a
14. a
15. c

Page 35. Word search

H	Z	C	C	R	H	L	N	V	C	X	Z	A	G	T
E	L	B	O	C	Z	X	A	Q	H	F	S	R	A	S
L	E	A	J	S	V	A	K	J	B	D	P	M	G	K
M	M	N	B	V	M	C	X	X	Z	L	K	S	A	J
E	H	G	F	D	S	O	A	P	O	I	U	T	R	Y
T	T	R	E	W	Q	A	N	S	D	F	G	R	I	H
Z	V	C	X	Z	R	F	D	A	S	D	S	O	N	S
L	K	J	H	A	S	W	E	R	U	T	Y	N	U	I
O	A	M	N	B	V	C	X	Z	L	T	K	G	G	B
F	G	L	O	V	E	S	D	S	A	P	O	R	E	O
W	Q	L	K	A	S	D	F	B	V	C	X	Z	S	O
T	Y	R	E	B	C	D	F	R	E	R	L	K	J	T
M	N	S	P	A	C	E	S	U	I	T	B	V	C	S
X	Z	L	K	J	H	G	F	D	S	A	A	P	O	I
U	Y	T	A	S	T	R	O	N	A	U	T	R	E	W

Page 36. Spot the difference

87

Page 39. What does an astronaut use this for?

It's a space toilet.

Page 42. Apollo capsule

B. 3

Page 43. Crossword

Page 46. Space connections

C and F

Page 50. 2. Flying skills

The runway is the correct place to land.

Page 52 Quiztro-nauts

1. 10
2. A frog
3. Taikonauts
4. In space
5. 1972
6. Laika
7. 1961
8. Valentina Tereshkova

Page 63. Word search

Q	E	T	X	U	O	A	F	**M**
G	J	G	D	Y	H	Y	F	**A**
F	**V**	**E**	**N**	**U**	**S**	I	S	**R**
P	**M**	**E**	**R**	**C**	**U**	**R**	**Y**	**S**
D	W	Y	F	Q	A	E	J	**M**
B	**J**	**U**	**P**	**I**	**T**	**E**	**R**	**O**
U	T	E	Q	N	V	X	K	**H**
F	S	Q	E	T	Y	**N**	P	**L**
K	H	G	F	D	S	**E**	L	**S**
N	B	V	C	X	Z	**P**	K	**A**
E	**A**	**R**	**T**	**H**	G	**T**	J	**T**
X	I	Y	D	C	F	**U**	R	**U**
V	H	V	C	X	P	**N**	I	**R**
Y	T	R	E	W	Q	**E**	Z	**N**
C	**U**	**R**	**A**	**N**	**U**	**S**	D	A
R	T	Y	U	I	O	Y	T	E

Page 64. Crossword

			M					
		V	E	N	U	S		
	J		T			A		
S	U	N		E	A	R	T	H
	P			O		U		
	I	M		M	E	R	C	U	R	Y
	T	O		A		N		
	E	O		R				
U	R	A	N	U	S			
				T				
				E				

Page 65. Solar System Quiz

1. Mercury
2. Neptune
3. Venus
4. Jupiter
5. Saturn

6. No
7. Star
8. Neil Armstrong
9. Mars
10. Gravity

Page 74. Find the alien!

TELE PORTALOOS

Page 76. Guess which of these isn't a real constellation

The Lawnmower. (Amazingly, all the others are real!)